# SERURUBELE POETRIES

### Katleho Kano Shoro

*Langaa Research & Publishing CIG*
*Mankon, Bamenda*

*Publisher:*
*Langaa* RPCIG
Langaa Research & Publishing Common Initiative Group
P.O. Box 902 Mankon
Bamenda
North West Region
Cameroon
Langaagrp@gmail.com
www.langaa-rpcig.net

Distributed in and outside N. America by African Books Collective
orders@africanbookscollective.com
www.africanbookscollective.com

*ISBN: 9956-762-19-9*

DISCLAIMER
All views expressed in this publication are those of the author and do
not necessarily reflect the views of Langaa RPCIG.

# Table of Contents

**Preface**................................................. vii
**Foreword**............................................... ix
**Acknowledgements**................................. xii

**Caterpillar Whims**................................. 1
Ode to Badimo le Baholo.............................3
Sesotho sa ka will not be written in italics.............4
Valued Conception..................................... 5
…IT… ..................................................7
Juicy, lekker, childish dreams...........................10
Tempted time...........................................12
Anthro Circle........................................... 13
Lay me close to your heart............................. 15
At First................................................. 16
FIRE CRACKER love............................... 17
Death by love.......................................... 19
Translations........................................... 22
Everything fell left and the world was the
right-side Up........................................... 23
I begged her to bleed..................................26
Lightning + sand = my wine glass....................27
Horror!.................................................. 28
While We Search for God............................. 30

**Cocoon Unwrapped**................................. 33
Born into It.............................................34
Blasphemy..............................................35
Morning is Broken..................................... 38
Bleeding Corpse....................................... 40
Truth Watered Down.................................. 41
absent performer.......................................43
Jack & Jill..............................................45
She Cried Rape…and I felt not enough...............47

iii

I want to meet you again.................................. 49
God was Never Here.................................... 50
Tasted tears in your name.............................. 52
Electing (role) Models.................................. 53
King of Mount Olive and Lady Peaches............. 55
I need you desperately.................................. 56
And then I was Woman and you remained
just a man................................................ 57
Encore.................................................... 58
sometimes i miss it..................................... 59
You left me.............................................. 60
Tears of Life............................................. 61
So I quit................................................. 62
Not enough to Just breathe........................... 63
House call to Mr Lucifer............................... 64

**The Fluttering**........................................ 67
O Serurubele!........................................... 69
Deliciously Beautiful.................................... 70
Carrier of Masculinity (Manly man)................... 71
We are...MOTION...................................... 74
Fabulous!................................................ 76
The Poet and her Habit................................ 79
Beads of Sweat...it's Summertime..................... 80
Wind and her Knickers................................. 83
Baby, I Cheated......................................... 85
Round. Pronounced. VoLuPTuOus................... 87
Spit Fire!................................................ 90
My Appeal............................................... 91
The Story of Women's Day............................ 94
(Lesbian) Right (in) to (Love) Freedom............... 99
The Heavens are pouring and staining............... 100

**Suckled From Between Flower Petals**............. 103
Peach Pit................................................ 105
She's coming back....................................... 108

You're cordially invited to sit next to me.............. 109

Pink.........................................................111

Little Miss Valentine.....................................112

Spinach Weed........................................... 113

Vintage.....................................................115

The past forever in the future.......................... 117

Passed Presently........................................ 118

RevolUtion...............................................120

A Prayer................................................. 122

You are not forsaken....................................123

baby Silence.............................................124

Dressed as Death......................................... 125

another Life gone.........................................126

Undoing MY Threads...MUST Be Crazy!...................127

Unpunctuated ending.................................... 129

It's not over 'til the Fat Lady Sings.................... 130

# Preface

Serurubele means butterfly in Sesotho. Dirurubele (butterflies) have inspired many a writer and have been the overtones, undertones or just slightly-featured tones in many pieces of literature - including some of the poems in here. Dirurubele in themselves are poetic; their lives are the ultimate tales of metamorphoses, radical change and possibility (the stuff poetries are made of), and their flight epitomises the ideals of poetry in motion and freedom. And then there is that infinite intermingling of colours and patterns...

Poetry comes in different forms and can never be patterned exactly the same particularly not in the way it is read, said or heard. Poetry means different things in different seasons to different people (whether it is, inter alia, experience, race, taste, language, gender or generation that makes these people different in light of that poem). The same poem can have multiple tones, be delivered in varying ways or coloured differently by a poet and an audience with every delivery. Hence Serurbele sena (this butterfly) having "poetries" (in plural).

Notwithstanding the possibilities and beautiful marvels found in the existences of Dirurubele and poetries, these two also speak to the limitations found in our realities. Butterflies and Poetries, especially poetries, can often illuminate the limits of our imaginations – sometimes even at our most imaginative. Both entities remind us that radical change and freedoms and summers where "butterflies rest easy" on sunflowers are not without losses, unfreedoms, responsibilities nor winter chills that see to the absence of even the petals between which butterflies suck their nectar.

Herein rest prose, poems, mumblings, performances pieces, convictions, poetic experiments, interpretations and reactions to life and some of its quirks, notables and muses. Some of these have hints of Sesotho (amongst other linguistic specks). Written over a span of about a decade, from the perspective of a young (South) African female who is no more than a caterpillar herself, the poems in *Serurubele Poetries* seek to playfully, seriously, honestly, and fictitiously live and breathe beyond just the writer's imagination because that's where many of them were formed and remain – beyond me. Still, I can only hope that these poems find some kind of relevance and find resonance with you…

**Katleho Kano Shoro**

# Foreword

> *I consider myself primarily a poet. I'm a poet in the African griot tradition, a keeper of the culture's secrets, history, short and tall tales, a rememberer. As a poet, I have a certain sense for language, both its beneficial and destructive powers. Therefore, as a writer who is well aware of his own cultural heritage, I am extremely affected by anything that alters that heritage.*
>
> Haki R. Madhubuti

The above quotation by the celebrated African American poet, Haki Madhubuti, is a claim that can be imputed to the young poetess, Katleho K. Shoro in her maiden volume, *Serurubele Poetries*. This title alone struck my curiosity to imagining the dazzle in the lines herein.

The good thing about poetry rest in the various opportunities it affords the poet/poetess to take the reader through the straight and crooked road life is. Katleho K. Shoro in *Serurubele Poetries* guides the reader into navigating this road which, only by so doing, does the reader like the poetess makes sense of a world in shambles or in a state of topsy-turvydom. Nonetheless, this poetess is not afraid to deconstruct the already deconstructed world she fends to understand. In so doing she clearly sees and portrays the binary of deconstruction and reconstruction as a necessary tool for humans to forge ahead in the chaos of this world. Such daring move is exemplified in "Anthro Circle" which in a Miltonian twist Katleho requests an interview be granted Lucifer to explain why he got fed up with God.

The poignancy and urgency in her lines summon the reader to fully appreciate her poetic scape filled with excitement and wonders. They are poems birthed from Katleho's obstinacy to uphold that which is of a child in her despite her being an adult. Espousing this approach of the famed French writer, Antoine de St. Exupéry, bodes well with a belief I have held as a poet for more than 30 years of writing. The said belief is that a poet/poetess is that adult who is capable of easily navigating between his/her world of adulthood as well as that of his/her childhood fantasies.

This volume blends contemporary colloquial text-messaging language with standard South African English as well as the Zulu language with the overall effect being a rhythmical collection from start to finish reflecting the polyphonous nature of the poetess' clime. This collection challenges the reducibility of poetry into any specific or particular folklore.

Some of the verses come across as prosaic. The reader need not be fooled by such for they uphold poetic rhythm with a sense of fascination. While cloaked in prose, those lines in the mouth, feel and sound, uncontestably like poetry exposing the poetess' fascination with navigation between the world as she knows it and the world of dreams.

The volume opens with "Ode to Badimo le Baholo" which turns out to be a note of /zik/ i.e. "sic" put to the muse. This revelation is found through darkness and ends with a note of the "light turned on" and it is one that requires many to keep it on us. Hers is a tableau of brightly coloured butterflies, both in sound and language, trapped in a political scape that only a message of peace and love to a world torn and still being torn apart by centuries of religious strife can guarantee any possible reconstruction.

Katleho's *Serurubele Poetries,* a 72 poems strong volume with mouthful verses, explores through a beguiling lightness of touch, her intimate conversation about and observation of love and hate, life and death, calm and violence, hope and despair, equality and inequality, justice and injustice, progress and stagnation, commitment and betrayal, machoism and womanism, etc. And the reader might even be amazed to find the poetess pre-empting the recent spate xenophobic violence in South Africa as she wonders in one of the poems if God was ever here, i.e. in South Africa.

**Bill F. Ndi (Poet and Critic)**

# Acknowledgements

Firstly, thank you to Langaa RPCIG for this amazing opportunity! Thank you to Professor Nyamnjoh for being more than a mere lecturer and supervisor: you are an inspiration, mentor, and my (academic) father. My parents, Pulane and Motale Shoro, ke a leboha for your endless support and encouragement in everything. Mama, thank you for editing Sesotho saka (it'll get there). A huge thank you to my family in general and Malome Malefetsane Ngatane and Mama Yvonne Kumalo, in particular, for believing in my poetic abilities before you could even be sure I had any. Mr. Welsh, you remembering the lines "I'm fabulous" encouraged me to continue writing and performing from high school.

*Poetry Delight* family. Some of my best writing (yet) has come from being inspired and pushed to be a more mindful yet adventurous poet by you! To my friends…I am thankful for all of you and to all of you! Tshepiso Mahlafuna you got me started. Khahliso Serei (and Mama Bathabile Serei) you were cheering me on at the beginning. Tiffany Mugo, Siphumeze Khundayi and Nicola Lazenby you never let me stop and thanks for the editing. Bulumko "Jelly Bean" Nyamezele, you're a constant reminder of artistic brilliance and humility…thank you for your consistent support. Dejavu Tafari (aka Vuyokazi Ngemntu), when I needed an extra set of poetic eyes, you, poet whom I respect, edited with honesty and care. Enkosi kakhulu!

Dankie to anyone who has ever asked me to perform or write and those whose works I have heard and read.

Badimo le Modimo: I am grateful for every muse created, I am grateful for words in abundance and thank you for my life and the ability to write. For me, it is through and within muses and wonders like butterflies, experience, histories, people and that which we *feel* that I believe Sacredness exists and the poetries of God(s) are illuminated.

# CATERPILLAR WHIMS
*Whims, unhindered proclamations,
naiveties and childish musings*

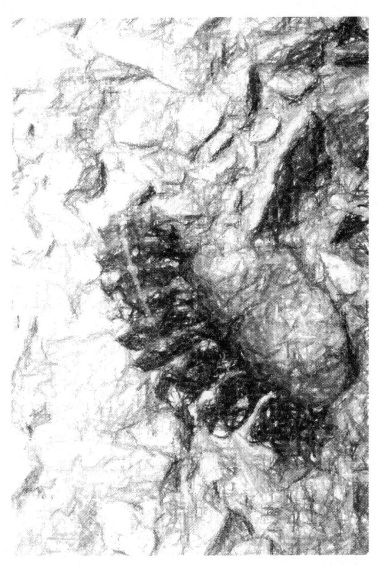

# Ode to Badimo le Baholo

We believe these are simply our own revelations,
that we found the light through complete darkness.

Really, there have been people in our corner
from the days we wore nappies.
People who began the process.
They hoped that this would be our revelation and our revolution.
These beautiful people bought the wires and the bulbs,
they taught themselves the art of electricians
and stocked up on electricity
so that all the foundation would be there for our light bulb moments. Then there are those who fed us carrots so we could navigate switches in the dark...

We think these are simply our own revelations.
It took many to turn the light on.
And there will be many to keep the lights on with us.

## Sesotho sa ka will not be written in italics

Sesotho sa ka will not be written in italics.
Next to English Sesotho sa ka, too,
will have her back up straight
because I have decided to make it
a "back-up-straight" kind of poem.

Sesotho sa ka will not be written in italics.
Not unless italics is the theme of the poem
or that exact line needs to
*slant so that when I recite it I know to lean back and emphasise*
hore...
Sesotho sa ka will not be written in italics.

# Valued Conception

HE coloured me gold.
Said I was good enough to wait until our jewels were ready to
grow and flow
and be more than foetus sippin' on amniotic fluid
waiting to exhale in drunken misery.
The silver lines intertwined
and we made more than happy;
We created a precious "him and I"
We added another circle to life
We stroked another piece of poetry to our delight
We waited before we gave this baby life.
By contracepting our minds
We saved another president from aborted life
Resurrected another Jesus who could have *just* died
Hell, through our foresight
we served humanity with another pair of insight.

SHE stroked the centre of my mere silver with her pure gold.
Scribbled strings of wisdom upon my womb
Made sure that our black and white footsteps in the golden
sands were in tune.
Ours was a plan so simple that its circles could not fit into
any boundaries
It was flawless,
All because she coloured me.

The HEs and SHEs may have coloured me
but it was I who conceived.
I conceived this jewel as a new testament of ME.
A revelation -

as clear as crystal yet purer than the golden streets paved
under the Red Sea.
And when I held this jewel in my arms,
I knew it was too heavy for me to take this task lightly.
Dumbfound –
by how its compacted complexities
beam unrestricted and brightly,
I'm still staring at my perfect piece of poetry.
Coloured by HIS hand,
Scribbled in HER imagery
And conceived through ME.

# ...IT...

IT sat humming a playful tune over its string of silent words
and when they heard IT they called IT philosophy.
so they philosophised around a fire that warmed their hunting
canine's intestines
they had named her Ruthy.
Ruthy had little to say but much to do with this extra-
ordinary capturing of pearls of words around a sea of fire
while IT sat humming playfully over...

IT philosophised.
IT spoke a folk language about a scientist's expertise.
IT might have forgotten to dot its i's and cross its t's
but even then they knew what IT means.
IT spoke before English struggled to capture Greek or Plato
(re)presented Socrates.
IT spoke of words as plain as the black stripes on the yellow
back of a bee,
the mere concept of Willy being free:
IT was adorned with simplicity.
It's through drinking from a calabash filled with ITS
simplicity
that they were left hung-over even before they had swallowed
their first sips.
You see, they knew exactly what IT meant before philosophy
helped IT move ITS lips
or science controlled the swaying of ITS hips
or IT found ways to hum poetry thru ITS finger-tips.

Ruthy growled to the open night,
asking the crescent moon not to shine so bright.

Ruthy swagged that tail like she had swagger,
allowing IT to suffocate even thoughts of parasitic fleas
and let IT dominate every strand of her fur coat.
Ruthy moved her shy self in a way that left the still air feeling like macking her
but the still air could not even make its way through her flea-less fur,
the still air had nothing to offer,
the still air could not court Ruthy or even let her know that it loved the way she moved.
It was the way Ruthy's silhouette captured the smile of the fire that made ITS simple humming a hum to be desired.

IT was captured that night IT sat humming a playful tune over its desirable string of words that warmed Ruthy's intestines and caused philosophising.
IT philosophised over a philosophy that captured her silhouette within the calabashes filled with simplicity.
When ITS words finally stopped being silent,
they concluded that in fact it sounded like folk, knowable philosophies
and so they called it poetry.
(and to this day even that poetry is absurd;
almost as wonder-filled as the light air supporting the soar of a bird
but not quite as lacking as the still air that could never mack Ruthy.)

But it seems they missed the point:
Even before ITS words made a sound and they found the name philosophy to describe and use IT,

IT was more than just knowable poetry and folk philosophies.

IT was swaggered by Ruthy,

IT inspired ITS naming

ITs poetry was only one of its parts hummed through ITS finger-tips

IT was never a folk language but spoke of such with humming ease and simplicity

IT was always…

IT.

# Juicy, lekker, childish dreams

Sometimes adults forget that we matter.
They tell us to dream as long as our dreams aren't too big and foolish.
They tell us to sing as long as we don't make a geraas with our songs.
They teach us to smile as long as our bright childish teeth don't distract them from being serious.
And when we play our songs and trudge through juicy dreams,
they remind us to wipe off our unexplained happiness along with the mud on our feet.

Other times adults forget that when we were too small to even speak,
they used to tell us secrets about how amazing love is
and how we can be anything we want to be as long as we believe.
But then we grow and ask questions and we're told that the future is ours
and so only in the future can we ever speak.
And even when we dream with our big fat healthy hearts,
they tell us to remember that it's all just make-believe.

I don't want to be an adult if it means that I forget how to sing and dream and be happy.
If that's how it's supposed to be,
I want to have grown up's body and the soul of a baby.
I want to make up songs and with other people who sing and believe just like me.
And then, when we become Oupas and Oumas

I want us to be able tell our grandchildren that the sky is NOT the limit because people have already landed on the moon!

But right now as a child,
I still want adults to remember that we children matter too.
Not only on June 16 but all the sunny mornings that God wakes us up to.
If our Creator made us strong enough to be kings and queens in heaven,
then our Creator must have left gold in our souls for us to be glorious on earth too.
I just want to be allowed to believe in impossible, lekker dreams that my holy brain was created to produce.

But since adults sometimes forget,
It's up to us to remember that we are beautiful and our dreams echo God's tune.
Our laughter and songs are the kinds that even God sings along to.
We, as children have to remember and believe that we don't only matter in our dreams.
Our Creator made us alive today and this is where our value should be.
I believe in me…

## Tempted time

U seduce Time into stopping against its better judgement.
U caress it in its doubt and sooth it into a state of enjoyment.
As U personify it into humanly defying universal laws,
it still rejoices
for Time itself has found opportunity to be off duty…
Defy its course.
Now Time who would have brought death's eventuality
no longer knows when death eventually will come.

## Anthro Circle

Catch him before he leaves.
Boil earl grey leaves and invite him for a game of croquet
before he closes his eyes,
before his guitar strings and those club lights remind him
that:
he's only a boy and he can't save the whole world...
not by the end of his song.
Still, let him sing.

Before you let him go,
spice his earl grey tea with scents of Care
and the Will to turn his tea-drinking experiences into fresh
new lyrics
about life in general
and its smells in particular.

Brew his cup in a way that makes steam whisper rumours
about
Adams of anthropology sacrificing their delectable ribs
in hopes that they'd somehow replace the missing cages with
vocal cords
that shape languages foreign to their ears
but are somehow knowable to their embodied experiences.

Ask him to write songs that complete concepts with the
stroke of a single string.
Remind him that -
the words sometimes sound best when he hums them
that our imaginations want to run and win races but our
words stand in our way.

Him humming would give them a chance to just Be.
Our imaginations want to run
but our imaginations want to run with *his* cords;
run in accordance with tunes spelt out by fingers on string
and a voice that floats in the air not letting words say a thing.

Ask him to persuade those strings to change the intentions of history:
to speak of Eves
to interview Lucifer and let him tell us why he got fed up working for God when God adored him so.
Maybe Lucifer will sigh in relief
and finally speak of caving-in under the pressure of being perfectly ordentlik
so he settled on being a weggooi-engel who could finally give into his sin
without feeling so bad about it.

Before we get ahead of the strings that have not started leading our imaginations...
Boil a few  earl grey leaves
And give that beautiful boy some of that tea before he leaves.

[For Laurie Sloan]

# Lay me close to your heart

Lay me close to your heartbeat.
Let me rock to the sound of chest expanding as lungs fill with
sweet air.
Help me close my eyes easy with your lulling caress across my
skin.

I breathe you…
And catch whiffs of parallel linkages between your existence
and my own.

Please,
do not speak of trivialities.
I'm scared of patheticisms tainting the sweet melody of your
perfect face.

Only with my eyes do I dare embrace you.
Only with my heart do I dare retrace imprinted memories of
your happy.

I'm scared,
trembling in my own thoughts about never wanting to let
harm slip past me and hurt you.
I can't even fathom having the audacity to speak of calamities
that may pierce your ears.

Before I put my armour on for you...
Lay me close and lull my heart with your beat.

## At First

It really just started with a prickle.
It wasn't too disturbing,
it just tingled… a little.
it was ok.
At first.

# FIRE CRACKER love

THE UNIVERSE LIT US UP!
match against match-box.
we were a pair matched for the moment.

match struck with first conversation.
no…match struck when I first walked in.
he saw me to my seat…with his eyes.
I ignored. BLEW it off.
but match was struck. FLAME LIT.
he came hither.
limited time to keep that FLAME ALIGHT. he used it well.
I listened. helped flame hasten to string.
FIRE CRACKER love LIT!

date one:
SUN was setting. we watched.
drank red wine. it settled into our shoulders. FUELLED our
eyes.
end of first date: no breathy kiss to BLOW out the flame.
the string was ABLAZE!

it only took a few seconds in the eyes of the universe to
LIGHT US;
one of its FIRE CRACKERS.
we were an EXPLOSION!
his red wrapped around my subtle blue and we both agreed to
EMIT ORANGE.
we held hands and closed our eyes.
our orange looked BRILLIANT!

with every heartbeat my ear caught while I lay on his chest,
my blue BURNT.
his red was perfect against the black sky,
against my need and vulnerability
and against me - the subtle blue to his red flame.
we worked...
IMPLODED into ourselves,
EXPLODED against that beautiful black night where we
learnt to be BRIGHT, together, in our darkest hours.
we EXPLODED MAGNIFICENTLY!
with every laughter and moan, the universe AMPLIFIED our
ERUPTION.

then. just as brightly as we RUPTURED the black sky into
MAGNIFICENT FLAMES,
just as LOUDLY as we entered its quietness,
we seized fire. burned out.
he could no longer sustain his red and I had no more blue,
neither of us had enough stamina to produce the orange and
our residual crackling halted too.

we were a pair matched for a moment.

# Death by love

Love asked her one question.
*LOVE* asked if she would lay herself on the line just to lick
*LOVE*,
have her tongue's tip move slowly down *LOVE*'s spine
before she died?
Every time, she replied:
*'It is my entire life that I am willing to sacrifice*
*just to have a moment to smother YOU between these arms of mine.'*

Persistently, she died at the hands of love.

Her version of *LOVE* was -
bathing in a pool of freshly squeezed strawberries that didn't
stain,
having the inside of her mouth showered with thick peach
juice without choking,
Irresistible love!

All she ever wanted was love.
Full cream, fattening sweet love
with a hint of mint.
The type that allowed her to wake up every morning
kiss her lover unashamedly
because the mint cured her morning breath
while the sweetness lingered on every last thought her lover
had before
leaving her lips to breathe.
It wasn't her lover she was after,
it was pure love.

She wanted love she could breathe-in with both nostrils,
before it seeped into her blood.
The kind that could take over her bloodstream,
lift veins to the skin's surface,
inspire hypothalamuses to utter excitement, and
instruct glands to make palms sweat.
The kind of love that you don't want escaping your pores
lest you never find it in you to breathe-in with both nostrils
again,
then, never have love-filled air charm your blood,
scare your sweaty palms into closing and clasp onto love.
It's not her lover she was after.
Her lover was merely the vessel of
pure unspeakable whispers that Love would hiss into her
drums
before beating sense out of her knees –
making them too weak to stand
or feel the millions of pins heating her soles.


She wanted love
Fanatically.
Obsessively.
Unwittingly, she let long-nailed, unclean fingers
occasionally claw into her back during her chase.
Every time she believed she possessed *LOVE*
she found herself washing off taintings,
disinfecting scars
and rebounding with pseudo-named love.
Persistently, she re-sowed *her* seeds of love
only to harvest the same fruitless imitation.
Occasionally, she would die at the hands of *her* love;
but she was reincarnated into different miracles

only to die at the hands of her same kind of love.

She needed *LOVE* to exist so hard.
She needed *LOVE* to sneak through the cracks of her window,
to place itself on the empty side of the bed that she left open and ready for *LOVE*.
But she was sure that full-cream, fattening sweet love with a hint of mint would one day balm the cracks on her lips with a morning kiss before and she could die satisfied.
That's why at the hands of a love pseudo-name she persistently died.

She kept being reincarnated into different miracles
only to die at the hands of the same kind of Love.

# Translations

Tell me love in your foreign language
I'll whisper you a smile in mine.
Hold my hand in two Latin syllables
I'll reciprocate by blowing onto you my state of mind.

I remember you….
You're that guy who said je'taime ka Sesotho
and had your interpreter translate your English accent with an
Arabic syntax.

Yes I remember you…
Distinctly.
You said you fell in love with the olive green you saw in
brown skin.
When I asked your opinions of politics
you replied in gibberish
saying that you don't speak of rubbish.

You sat me down on your thigh;
covered in Greek mythologies
reminiscent of Zulu royalties.
You explained to me, thoroughly,
how the Shona were engulfed in the arms of the Beti
when they fell in love with the Chinese.
And when you arb'ly mentioned how
the Swati sailed ships built in Aborigine castles of literature,
I enjoyed you utterly.

So here's a thank you kiss
blown in the language of appreciation.
I hope you manage to translate it.

# Everything fell left and the world was the right-side Up

The mighty celestial being held the earth on the tip of his second finger,
spinning it slightly so that his little human lemmings would think it to rotate.
He spun and used his nostril hairs to keep it spinning
and sometimes when he spun it too fulfillingly
the entire earth would feel a little dizzy
and do something mischievous just to restore balance
to how great the feeling left them feeling
the time after the spinning left them dizzy.

One light second, when this mighty celestial being
- whose name occupies not the entire notion of his existence
but only explains the might of his baby toe -
this light second changed plenty for the mischievously spinning lemmings
who beat egg whites into meringue splashed with specks of lemon.
In this light second, this celestial being spotted his own shadow
but mistook it for a dazzling creature
he didn't remember tapping his thumbs against a harmless black hole to conceptualise.
And he remembers all but still managed to mistake his own shadow for this creature that looked like it came in the form of a being wrapped in this metallic ring of stars
that had to have been the basis of Saturn's splendor before.

In trying to look back to examine the dazzling creature,

the celestial being's nostrils brushed over a dusty planet and he sneezed.
Sneezed so hard that the earth tilted in its spin and every lemming fell on their left side causing left concussions everywhere.
Everywhere!

The moon rocked to the left,
taking the ebbs with it
Dragonflies that had been drowned on the right side
for two decades shorter than a light second
escaped into the sky and glided on lopsided sunrays.

Chaos! Pandemonium!
All this ensued as the scientists of great theories issued a statement claiming how it was the right time for the right side of the brain to dominate...and naturally they said this using paint.

Chaos! Havoc!
All logic tilted to the one side as people started replacing maths with the study of emotions twice removed and physical science only included physical chemistry.
People used their brains from the right and never quite reached the left.

The celestial being picked the dust from his nostril hairs,
throwing the specs into another universe
since he now knew that the creature was in fact the shadow
he kept as company before he started his earth-spinning
he turned his attention back to the lemmings.

To restore balance all he did was let the lemmings sit on
blank canvases
while he fed them fruity, bright purity.
They all grew up to live creatively.

# I begged her to bleed

I begged her to bleed:
To make her point so distinctly
that all that would exist is torn pieces of her victory.
I just needed her to say something…
even if it was just letting out her mo(u)rning breath-
it didn't have to be sweet.
I had to slit her wrists for her
because I wasn't sure she was alive
(can't imagine when she would have had the time to die).
All I needed was a tear:
not much,
just a staining pain that would threaten to crack the seal of
her insane silence.
But she refused.
Refused to be beaten into talking,
charmed into smiling,
taught into feeling.
She wouldn't hear of life.

This damn pen refused to write.

# Lightning + sand = my wine glass

Shit happens.
Toilets stink up.
Nappies overflow
and underwear gets greased up.

But look
my wine glass possibly came from this beach sand.

It gets hard.
Your brain gets stuck between solid ruts,
your feet get soaked even though you're sure of a sole
and little stones climb up the smoothness of your feet as you
step.

But look
I'm drinking wine from a glass that lightning made out of
sand.

Sometimes fuzz is the buzz word.
Your body feels too worn to help you stand straight.
Your back arches so far back you hear unhealthy clicks
and your hands tremor at the horror of arthritis creeping up
as your whole being burns from devil-hot to carbon-ice-
sizzling.

But look
wine smells like guava
and I'm drinking it out solidly electrocuted sand glass.

# Horror!

At first:
I cried. She cried.
We cried for it was said to be a tragedy.
The part where he died had our hearts sunken to our knees
because it couldn't be!
Then the prequel explained.

Suddenly...

He died and it thrilled me.
She SAW 2.
The horror silenced lambs
that were born to become sheep
that jump over fences
while the sweaty man - with clogged nostrils –
tried to grab onto sleep.
But…
because the lambs could never make sounds that lull him to sleep
and invite him into a world ruled by Freddy,
he hid in the closet.
Feeling more trapped than midgets bound to bed-posts
with unforgiving leather straps,
He waited…
hoping that Chuck Norris would finally leave his action
to save him from the horror-world
that brewed the likes of Chucky.
He held his breath for what seems like a time long enough for
black spiders to form webs around the next generation of
[horror]star-wars

that would end in either complete darkness or multiple skywalkers
breathing creepily on our necks as we closed our eyes tightly.
While he held his breath
what really happened is that the spider-men spun webs around his nose and mouth
and soon, he fell into a sleep deeper than he'd wished.

There...
he had eternal fantasies about being an incredible hulk
that even invisible fantastic heroes gravitated towards.
I'm sure somehow in his final destination, he was happy
but still...
I chocked on the sight of cobwebs knitted across his face
and it did more than just thrill me.
and because she SAW 2, she could confirm it was more than a tragedy
so we both sat in horror.
Waiting in suspense…

# While We Search for God

While I was searching for my God
I looked up at you
Every time I did I would feel better
Never realised that until now.

While you were searching for your God
You would always have your hand squeezed by your baby boy
and for some reason the anxiety you felt seconds before
was squeezed out of you
You never realised until now.

While he was searching for his God
His grandfather always disturbed his wonderings with the knocking of his hammer on wood
One day, while God was still being sought after and wondered about
his grandmother smiled,
calmingly, rocking on the chair his grandfather's wood and hammer
had sculpted and bound and sanded together.
He never realised until then.

While they were searching for their God
They did so together.
They found comfort in each other.
They prayed and knelt and hoped to find God together.
They never let each other give up the search.

While we search for God we find pieces of him in each other
and ourselves

While you search for your God please praise the one that lives within.

# COCOON UNWRAPPED

*Growing, conceding, discovering cynicism and morbidity*

## Born into It

Born into it.
Right into the brown past the green of it.
Right there where it's too precise to mistake it for anything
else.
Born into its colour, its mood, its smells, its food...
Everything that makes it IT
and you're a part of it.

But nothing about it - or you - says that you have to remain
into it.
Yes, you're born into it but...
if you move closer to the left, you might catch a different
whiff,
if you move closer to the right, the mood there may alter your
palate;
change your perspective.
and if you venture closer to the top,
you may just see the green and what lies beyond it.

There's nothing wrong with being born into it.
There's nothing you can do to change being born into it.
You were born into it,
and if you so please you can remain into it.
But nothing about it or you says you have to remain in(to) it.
So if you so wish, move in any direction away from it
and you may begin to alter being into it.
But it's not all or nothing:
YOU may take, leave, add on what it means to be...
born into it.

# Blasphemy

Bow down and praise me.

I am that religion that came as a delicious dream,
I am that God that came via false missionaries that led you to
your slavery.
I am the truth that helped you forget the truth and now
Badimo ba lona ha le khone ho ba peleta
empa laka lebitso le tswa ka dinko tsa lona tse se para,
dinko tse fapaneng ho bona bale who fed you a manuscript
that conveniently inscripted their rights to trade you,
as long as the name of God they used.

God.
Ke tla re Modimo ke mang when I know the word God?
Naweza kumujua Mungu when I know the word God?

God, I wish I knew you true then I wouldn't be blasphemous
in this bitter tune.
God, I wish I could pray and believe that the "Our Father"
makes ghetto dreams come true.
You see my granddaddies, they bartered everything they had
in exchange for you,
the same god who had them swinging to the blues and
singing "Amazing Grace"
how sweet the sound of that freedom that they will never
taste.
I too proudly verbalise Oxford's definitions of a freedom but
when it comes to annunciating its meaning, ho peleta is a
mother!
So keep your notions of a freedom and give us our free.

Keep your stories of a lightly-tanned Jesus until you realise that your history of my ancestry is a recognisable part of me.

But I realise that as past native, I messed up!
I failed to see that the Holy Bible was their trick and their treat.
I failed to inhale the lines in between that covered up sexism, slavery and rights to superiority.
Even as past native woman I longed to be a Virgin Mary, forgetting to question whether I'd still be leader of that story if Joseph could have babies biologically.
So as woman I took the blame: I am a descendant of an Eve who twisted an Adam's arm to put her apple in his mouth, between his teeth.
But I dare not speak of the slippery, sly male angel serpent who snuck up behind an Eve to help her discover her sexuality because that, even I realise, is blasphemy.

But Ndaneta!
I'm just tired of living in the hope that my death will one day bring significance to my life.
Ek is net 'n bietjie gatvol of being pumped full of daai man se conspiracies and theories about religion bettering *my* life.
Too many people die IN THE NAME OF JESUS. AMEN! Amen?

Too many believers' intestines are sacredlessly exploded, left to dry -,
their holy wars led them onto landmines.
Too many worshippers die,
believing that detonating their insides
will help free another man's mind.

I don't know about you but I get a little affected when I see babies
being turned into refugees, needing to run and hide in hills
because they're being killed softly
whether they're ready or not to believe in *anything*.

I'm not saying I know everything or even anything,
I'm just saying:
Before you hate me because I'm Christian,
Terrorise me because I'm Muslim,
Doubt me because I'm pagan
Or fear because voodoo is my religion
Can you first look at me as if I was human?

## Morning is Broken

Morning forgot to break into the night
and now the black bird isn't speaking because it is still
without sight.
Morning is broken.

Morning is broken
So the mourning of the night continues...
Tears are still being cried from last night
Blackness is still wrapped around the shoulders of those who
await morning to stop their crying.
The morning sun has not burnt the tear tracks to make them
shy
so they continue to cry...

Morning is broken.
And it is breaking the strength of the night.
Night cannot go on forever.
Never mind their inability to forever mourn,
and produce tears
and have their backs curled to accommodate how close their
knees need to be to their chests.
The night just can't go on forever.

It is in sleeping during the day
that night is able to be so powerful
so as to dismiss the sun
and illuminate the moon that gives them the tears and
strength to cry without being shy.
It is in gathering all its thoughts during the day

and sometimes allowing the moon to shine so brightly that all their tears come out in a single bout - that's what being night is about.
So night cannot be there during the day.
Yes while it sleeps it farts out shadows
but that is part of the order of things;
that is part of night's resting
so that night is able to calm souls and let people let go
when the day has finally decided to read a book on its time off.

Morning needs to break into this night.
Mourning needs to be broken
so that backs can be upright
and courage can be attempted before night allows them, again, to cry.
Night needs to remove itself from the black bird's eyes,
Night needs to dismiss the moon so that they may have too little strength to cry,
Night needs to sleep and fart out shadows and allow them to day-dream and be free of blackness tightly wrapped around their shoulders
- their cloaks need to be washed and dried for the night anyway.

Morning needs to stop being broken and just break into the night already.
Night needs to sleep.

# Bleeding Corpse

The mortuary failed to keep its sheets clean.

Clean whites constantly stained with
deep,
thick
red
every time a relative came close to the corpse
and felt.

The corpse -
young,
full,
with the ability to pick up on warm relative blood -
failed to stay cold just like it failed to stay alive.

The mortuary couldn't keep its sheets clean.

Every time life walked by,
blood warmed,
unclogged itself,
scars burst open
leaving blood to do as it pleased to the white sheets.

The mortuary failed to keep the sheets clean
Corpse refused to stop bleeding.

## Truth Watered Down

You
slipped
through my fingers
and dripped, carrying
loads of my salt and fear,  anxiety,
and seasonal wishes of you being here.
Even then,
as I watched you
slip through, it sounded as if
you said you were holding onto me
but then you took the leap.
You
told me
I could hold you.
And my palms curved;
I brought all my fingers together
and squeezed the air from between each one.
They
all stood there,
all five fingers pointing
their dirty dry nails to the air
while curving their waists to hold you in place;
in my palms. Everyone was waiting for you to arrive
and stay. But you slipped
through my fingers.
You
caressed every one of my fingers
before abandoning them with a smirk on your face
and intention to
drip

and
be
wasted
only
tasted.

You
were never
 going to cleanse them, were you?
Your intentions were never to hold conferences
with my dirty nails until you'd made your point so precisely
that air was the only thing left for them to debate about
inviting.
You were never going to quench me were you? You were
never going to stay
in the middle of my palms long enough to have me drink you
through my cracked lips and feel you
sliding down the back of my throat
after winking at my
shrivelling
palate.
You
were never
mine to have and to hold.
ALL you did was slide down the spines of
my tense, curved fingers to remind me that I couldn't have
you.
Yet, I need you. Dear Water I need you more desperately
than I need
the sky from which you are meant to fall. But as it turns out
the national treasure isn't for all.
Not at all.

## Absent Performer

It had been a while
since I meant the words that I'd written
with intention and feeling
and once upon a time meaning.
I had memorised my lines so finely
I did not have to think about them,
I just said them.
They slid out so easily;
following the smooth, muddy path
that other words had left behind
as bitter winds of trying-to-remember
made their reign fall on them side-ways.
I didn't even need to take the time out to recall
the feeling that came with the words,
even that was embodied in my remembering them.
Gestures that were established
in the first few tries of muttering individual lines
stuck.
They were embodied in the text that had stained my memory.
A thick, jelly-like stain that had body and colour and
presence…
A stain nonetheless.
Even my smile was so rehearsed,
it came off as genuine,
not saying that it wasn't genuine
but I don't recall the feeling that created these words
so I'm not sure if this smile is still as real as it used to be
when I was stumbling over the words at first.

I anticipated the audience clap.
As usual,
I marked my territory by employing the identity of the shy girl
who found her confidence when she grasped the mic
and grabbed her voice from the back of her consciousness.
I anticipated the audience being right there where I no longer
was.

But just as I got on stage and started the unholy ritual of
reciting rehearsed tunes and talking out a love song
I spotted a couple kissing in the little gontjie of a dark corner;
unphased by my stage presence and rehearsed act,
kissing as if I was their audience.
Those two sucking face at back, back, back, back
made me feel my words again, for the first time.
They made me remember what I owed my audience…
my presence.

# Jack & Jill

You can ask me but I don't know Jack...
who went up the hill,
got raped by Jill
and no-one's seen his soul still.
All the king's horses and all the king's men
didn't believe that Jack, being a cock
could be violated by Jill, the hen.
But it happened
Again and again...


little Jack found comfort in his pen running down through his veins
and threatening to one day commit him to a suicide
but until then, behind Peter his pumpkin eater, he'll hide.
Little Jack would rather his daily meal be taken from his mouth
by the manly Peter
than in any woman confide.
So, under the shadow of fat Peter's pumpkin crack he hides;
turning his back to any object within which
a reflection of his distorted self he might find.
He watches the twinkle-twinkling little stars
as he withstands the prickling of cleaning his own scars,
thinking maybe it wouldn't be this hard
if Jill wasn't as deadly as Venus
and he didn't theoretically come from a Mars.
He looks at the moon
hoping his cow will jump over soon.
Every night, before in Jill's sick sweat he lies,
and in the potent sounds of her breathing he cries,

he imagines himself to be Gorgy-Porgy getting another man's
pie
but it never helps, especially when he starts to cry.
Most of his tears recite "Mary had a little lamb" -
wishing Jack was the little lamb
never to be slaughtered with the object that enters him from
Jill's right hand.
Most of his saltless tears are filled with
the desperate, bleeding yolk that escaped Humpty-Dumpty's
shell
as he fell
(off the wall his mother told never to climb atop to begin
with).
If Jack had love for a mother instead of a sweating Jill,
he reckons he'd be a force to be reckoned with.


This one special night
Jack begins to giggle-gaggle-wiggle-and-waggle
and through his hysterical laughter
he grabs the farmer's wife's butcher knife
and becomes the flood that causes the insy-winsy spider to
fall.
Thrill!
Jack imagines it to be the drops of his soul
rolling down that hill,
drowning the sweat and sounds of Jill.
He feels mother Jill orgasm to his scream
as his heart pounds fast only to beat…still.
She peaks;
climaxing to blood, and veins and…thrill.
Jack never came back alive from that hill.

# She Cried Rape…and I felt not enough

She sat me down on a two-seater rock
and in between hyper-ventilations and spotting bare-footed
humans trying to turn daisies into lilies.
She cried rape.
She was a friend of mine
but even then I failed to picture what the tears would be like
if rape was the subject matter of my cry.
She sat me down on a two-seater rock
and I wished the music in the background provided the
fitting dramatic sounds
to make me *feel* what she was saying.
I needed to pull Jesus aside while he celebrated his octave
and ask him to remind me how to be Christian again
long enough for me to start praying…
for her.

I couldn't understand her.
She explained it in plain tears,
yet I still couldn't fully conceptualise what I was hearing.
Yes, I know about metaphors and similes.
I know how to imagine gay dragons never hurting the
princess
because thoughts of seeing her one man army
charms the fire out of their breath.
I fully comprehend that fairytales are really politics
and those who aren't perfect beauties are moulded into three
sisters with blisters
or Edwards with scissor-hands.
I even know that he sinned when he stole a bite from the
apple between her skinny thighs.

What I'm saying is that I get a lot of things easily…
But her emotions I couldn't seem to understand.

Maybe if we went back and synced the fall of her tears
with drops from my beer,
I would cry over spillage or
the two liquids would dissolve our two-seater rock
and when we were finally swimming in the same texture of mud,
the salt from her tears would dry on my skin
and my blood would be intoxicated into feeling.
Maybe if I had closed my eyes hard enough
I could have lost myself in darkness
and created nightmares similar to the realities that flash about in her mind
whenever she cries.
I'm sure there was a way I could have frustrated myself into understanding forceful friction
or at least feeling something.

But I couldn't feel anything.
Even now as I sit on my one-seater bench,
surrounded by untainted daisies,
I can't seem to grasp the notion of feeling raped.
Sometimes I wished she had sat someone else down on that two-seater rock;
someone who could have at least been able to cry and empathise.
All I could do was listen and lie:
I told her everything was going to be alright.
I can only hope that it ever becomes alright.

# I want to meet you again

I want to meet you again.
No revisits.
No "remember those times"…
I just want to be reacquainted with you. Anew.
A fresh, new air that would fill these same lungs the same way
the last fresh air did.

I want to meet you again.

Skip the formalities and just go straight into the friendship;
the knowing yet the unravelling mysteries.

I miss the new you.
I just hope "new you" will come soon
because it's lonely just standing in this smooth desert of old
me
smiling that I'm alive but…

Yeah, really, it would be swell if you popped by.
It would be nice to meet you again.

# God was Never Here

We waited.

No, they waited.

(I refuse to be associated)

Even my limited, one-sided knowledge of African history lets me know that

God was never here.

Stop asking why he has forsaken you, dear foolish ones.

He was never here.

God did not forsake this dark continent,

The idea of what we…they…thought he'd bring did.

God was never here.

I know that by how he apparently landed on this continent and what he apparently left behind when he decided to commit to only one bond in some lavish European country whose broadcasted barbarism is further in the past than Africa's.

God was never here.

Not the God whose spelling we're…they're…barely able to articulate anyway.

Maybe he never came because they didn't call him right.

Maybe his eyes enjoy light more than they do the darkness and night.

Perhaps God likes shiny objects made by man from all the resources he's provided,

and that bloats his ego and adorns his peckish altar just right.

God was never here.

He never came, he didn't want us, he prefers masterpieces over us…them…

drafts.

If he ever came, he didn't like us…them…very much.

They waited.
And when they died by the hands of their rebellious
teenagers;
faces overthrown by translucent shades,
mouths frothing with pointless ambitions,
and fingers clutching on shiny technologies.
When they died there,
I hope they realised
*that*
God never came.

## Tasted tears in your name

I tasted tears in your name.
Raised my cheek and heard my heart chant a "prost" in your honour, or lack thereof.
I cried for you.

# Electing (role) Models

They told me to zoom into my future.
All I saw was Mother Future (tense) tied up
about to be raped and de-frauded of her integrity
right after she released a solo album
where   toy-toying   is   the   new   kwaito-dance   for   the
unemployed.
Their intellect, I guess, she had employed.

No role models.
In them, I have no role models.

They told me to cope with my present
I found myself cutting ribbons of virginity
on the clean white sheets of potential presidency.
Down with integrity!
ALL the way down:
below the belt,
above the depths of peace
but under the pants of promiscuous leaders
who, from the urges of their genitals lead.

No role models.
In them, I have no role models.

Only peace found is pieces of meat
they find in little girls
while bellowing at boys to style up and gain some pride…
suddenly.
From nowhere really.

No role models.
In them, I have no role models.

I have models…
Models of sexuality blasted onto my daily sun,
creating shadows that swallow up all tales of youthful, bright futures.
Blinding.
A bloody black-haired bimbo is what they encourage me to be
as their dominatrix over me bruises my belly brutally.
Now I birth aborted stories of pride
and distorted pictures of disabled histories:
the models' histories.

My elected (role) models:
they model histories…with a tick from me.

[11 March 2009]

# King of Mount Olive and Lady Peaches

King of Mount Olives had a kink to his smile.
Lady Peaches thought the kink was cute –
it tickled, like the idea of kiwi falling within the canned
colony.
Only when King of Mount Olive's own thoughts made him
so happy…
he exposed his olive-stained front teeth,
that she realised -
the kink in his smile was the disguise of an upside-down,
worn-the-wrong way-round, frown…
directed at her.
Poor Lady Peaches:
now she'll probably have to conform to making fruit salad
babies with exotic guavas.
Lady Peaches will never see her glorious idea of peaches and
olives on one pizza base
ever coming true.

# I need you desperately

I need you desperately.
I need the pending, fought and fallen tears to mean something.
I need you desperately.
I need to know that I was lonely for something
I was meant to be having, wanting
and so desperately in need of,
that I willed the universe to get it for me
and recognised its scent as soon as it turned my corner...toward me.
Sometimes I ask to be alone
but never lonely.
Sometimes I fight company
but I never said I wanted company to stop wanting me.
I need you desperately
Almost painfully.
Not sure what exactly you are
but you have to be worth the tears, the lonely, the belief that it will be okay.
Don't know what's not okay but something isn't.
Not sure where I am not but I will get out of here to there.
I need you desperately.
Be you a dream,
be you a revelation,
be you the company that saves me from lonely…
I need you desperately.

# And then I was Woman and you remained just a man

I was a woman and you were a man.
I had breasts and responsibilities
And you suckled, sucked, drained and left me with yours.

And then I was a Woman:
Accepting, responsible and dry (but alive)

But you remained just a man:
Freely giving me more to accept and be responsible for
and since it wasn't enough that I was dry
and it was certainly too much that I was alive
you, man, tore through me,
felt your muscle bulk as you watched me bleed,
and even sucked the last bit of blood before you wiped off
your lower lip
with your soiled dipper.

Even without breath I remain a Woman
(If not more)

And you...
even with your life (and mine dead between your lips and
thighs and palms)
...remain just a man
(Even Men deserve more)

# Encore

**He's not fighting for you…**

*"Encore! Encore! Encore!"*
He spoke with a tight-fisted tongue and spat out punch-lines
that left her ears bleeding onto her insides.
Inside,
she had word-burns from how he dragged her worth across
heaps of harsh-textured words.
He had hurt and bruised her with nouns and adjectives,
and her silence echoed "Encore" that turned them into verbs.

**Yes he's fighting…**

*"Encore! Encore! Encore!"*
His fist shouted an "encore" to his foot as it landed in her
ribs and…
Crack.
Surely she must have died with that Matrix style, super-phly,
Kung-fu kick
phela last time she fell down with only a smack.

**But the war is waged against you.**

## sometimes i miss it

sometimes i miss it.
and when i do
it always comes when long hours of thought and mundane,
far-stretching landscapes meet the calmest part of me.
i don't know how to make the mountains look smooth
or make that feeling feel like a blessing.
i just don't know how to stop missing
and drenching it in salty thoughts.
just when i thought the blue sky meant wholeness…
i go and miss it.

# You left me

Deur ons' oë het ons' siele ontmoet
en dit was al wat ek wou gehou
Maar die hemels het hulle hekke oop gemaak.
Al wat ek kan nou doen is asem vang
met geen punt om te lewe.
Jy was my rede om te lewe.

You left me.

If my evaporated tears filled the skies
asking you to come back to this life of mine
would you even try?
Mother you left scared,
Daddy, nothing else could compare,
Brother, I miss the times we shared.
You left me.
And this is my life after your death.

# Tears of Life

I cried.

Wept until my wet tears fell onto my soft, dry palm
Ka fuparela dikeledi tsaka ka seatleng, 'cos
For the first time I understood what it meant to have life but
not be alive.

So I had to watch my tears to understand this from without,
too.

## So I quit

My heart breathed to the beat of its footsteps.
I smiled at his laugh
and stepped to her path.
I fell, followed, allowed my-self to be swallowed in its hollow being.
But I was BEING and that's all that mattered.

So I carried on BEING
while it sucked at my being's blood
and sucked until all that was left was the shape of the ribs he apparently gave to me.
But he wanted them back.
She, too, sucked and chewed.
No longer were my enzymes necessary because she became my metabolism;
sucked and chewed all flavour out of me.
I was dying for just BEING.

But with what was supposed to be my last breath,
I proclaimed "I quit".
I quit.
I quit!
Out of my coma I followed and for once I stopped just BEING.
Because I was tired of *just* being, I QUIT.
I QUIT!

# Not enough to Just breathe

It's not enough to just breathe.
It's not enough to just quietly expand lungs over bladder until bladder threatens to combust and burn shame down cotton whites.
It's not enough to sigh only under warm sheets.
It's not enough to just add a full stop.
If an exclamation mark isn't there,
only a comma will do.
It's not enough to just breathe.

# House call to Mr Lucifer

She made a house call to dear Mr. Lucifer
telling him not to worry 'cos she'd found her soul;
neatly wrapped up in serene metallics
it was imprinted with the kind of wonder that butterflies are dipped into
before heaven releases them into the day sky.

And these butterflies…
They know nothing of the colour that drips from leaking wounds
or the notion of blood stains.
These butterflies have turquoise melodies flowing through their veins.
And there…
settled between the creases of their bright orange, indigo patterns
are delicious lavenders that tell tales of Beauty falling in love with the Beast
and holy scriptures calling what Mary and Joseph created some kind of holy trinity.
(All it is really is, is that they'd rediscovered those butterflies that make the soul happy).

So…
She had to make that call to dear Mr. Lucifer,
and she knew the number 'cos she had him on speed dial.
Constant Redial.
Lucifer used to wrap his big, bold, red arms around her existence
until she was suffocated of all life.

Her precisely-proportioned, lightly peachy petiteness
always looked so disturbingly picturesque when she lay there.
She would lay in this foetal position;
the subtle soft skin of her delicate body in absolute contrast
with the thick red that lay beside, between and inside her.
(see) Mr. Lucifer begged her to bleed.
He took petite bites out of her sanity
and made sure that every night she confirmed her loyalty
by having her flesh French kiss the ripples of his sharp blade
so deeply
that thick, red blood made love to her arms
before lying in the picture of disillusion beside her.

It's the only way she knew how to live.
And as if the potent smell chanted a song of immortality
in cautious whispers,
she smeared the thick red all over her body,
in slow strokes
and low hopes
that if she perhaps didn't die,
at least some of the pain in her life
was controlled and bled through the morbid pleasures of her
eyes.
She lived to bleed
and in so doing she held hands with the devil
on a rusted merry-go-round that left splinters cutting through
her feet.

She lived to bleed
until one day she met a woman who used paper mache to
carve out colorful contrasts.

She, too, had lived by the blade engraved with bloody
intentions
until she discovered that she could use wet strips of paper
mache
that meant nothing in particular
and from them she sculptured a picture of day courting night
and when the two had given birth to dusk it dawned on them
that even when insomniac crescent moons didn't appear in
their daytime,
happiness could still be reflected through butterflies.

So that day,
she made a house call to dear Mr. Lucifer
telling him not to worry cos she'd found her soul
neatly wrapped in serene metallics
that recite verses of salvation coming from a wonderfilled
butterfly-kind of happy.

Through notions of butterflies she rediscovered her soul's
happy.

# THE FLUTTERING
*It is playful, experimental, confident, and in motion*

# O Serurubele!

the cocoon opened,
the caterpillar that lived before you was no more
and you,
Serurubele,
you spread the oranges and indigos of your wings
and you were gone.

wind wrapped under your wings
and your ambitions took flight in a direction out of sight.

you were gone.

you can never be ungone
be that caterpillar
be cocooned
be how you were known.

o Serurubele
now a thing of the sky
of wings and winds
of bright orange and indigo patterns
of flight

o Serurubele!

# Deliciously Beautiful

You're deliciously beautiful.
Your heart must be sculptured in the shape of a pit-less peach
'cos all I ever want to do is dip you easy in my mind's cream
Take petite bites out of you…slowly
so I can savour the scent of your being.

You imbue me,
make my skin want to turn itself into a fountain of golden caramel
'cos only you have mustered the texture of dark chocolate.

Explain to me - in whiffs of delicious -
how you're able to hold the sun in your right hand
and have the sea beckoned at your feet,
yet the two never realise that even before picturesque sunsets
they meet in YOUR BEAUTY.

Your kind of brilliance overflows from calabashes of watermelon shells
but never touches the ground because I crave even your left overs.
I would dive, fall, and scrape both knees just to get a taste of thee.
Red bush leaves shrivel and die at the sight of even your past
for they know that only you are worthy of nourishing me.

Nourish me…beautifully.

You're deliciously beautiful.

# Carrier of Masculinity (Manly man)

Manly Man
My Modern Marvel
Master of My Musical Melody
Maker of Myths and Make-beliefs
yet Maestro of Mathematical Mysteries
He exists...Magnificently
This Man
Mobile of Masculinity
Magnum opus is his Muscular Machinery that he names
Marginal
but I believe his Mind to be Magical
This Man carries the Mind of Machiavellis
Manners of Martyrs like Ghandis
and a Mouthpiece of Merit like Martin Luther and other
Kings
Like the Mockingbird
Multiple Mad Melodies to My feMininity he sings
This Man gives My Mind Marijuana wings
I love me some Manly Man!


MANLY MAN:
Possessor of only a left rib because he gave up his right
so I could be sculptured into who I am.
Carrier of those ridiculously strong hands
that cup mine so precisely
that he only can understand how to instil calm into my blood
by merely caressing my palm.
My heart beats in the palm of his hand.
This man.
He is my sunshine and he rises.

Oh, dear Sunshine,
he rises and shallow sea waves evaporate between his smile.
I think dear Sunshine has forgotten to stop smiling
'cos his constant blaze keeps my precipitation forming.
My appreciated global warming:
melting my heart when trifling boys turn it as cold as ice
and my hatred for males is M.O.P deep
he rescues me and takes me into his arms
and lets my heat beat in his palm.
My soul sleeps in the palm of his hand.
My heart beats to the rhythm of the name of this Man.

I speak not of a male who thinks like a boy;
'Gugile umzimba but he still has little girls and boys
running around his Beemer toy.
Hayi, ngikhuluma ngendoda yamampela bo.

Manly Men exist.
But I speak of a specific man.
No other man so beautiful has called me "Baby" and made
my soul smile.
Not even a song composed by a heavenly Barry White, sung
by the spirit of a Luther Vandross and played alongside the
trumpets of a Louis Armstrong.
Not even *that* song can hold a tune more beautiful than this
beautiful man calling me "Baby" and making my soul smile.

I adore this father of mine!
He's shown me best how to own being human
(not sure if he can fully understand this concept within
himself 'cos my Daddy is superhuman.
My superman.)

Ntate, kea ho leboha for existing as the epitome of being the carrier of masculinity.

Thank you for all those times my feet couldn't carry me
because my eyes caught a case of sleep in front of the TV
and the next morning I'd awaken magically in my Tweedy nightie
and still have my virginity.

Too many little girls tell the story of having their trust raped from them while their hymens are ripped into drip-dropping blood pouring out as her pureed innocence stains the white of her little panties.

So I thank you Daddy.

If God exists, to me he exists through you.
If the concept of Botho seizes to persist,
I've rediscovered it in you.
I'm a proud wearer of my Daddy's genes.
Nothing as au fait as Versace, my Daddy's label is me.
My Daddy: Manly Man and Carrier of Masculinity.

## We are…MOTION

We are…
MOTION.
A traffic-less jam
vibratin' frequently under passenger seats
'til you annoy yourself into being delighted in our beat.
We beat caution into skipping danger and giving us a free
pass at every intersection.

We are…

The passion that roars the engine of genuine proposals
when he steps on the pedal asking you to "Be My Wife"
and you hum that you will travel with him 4 by 4 times 'til
you re-volvo around eternity
and create the innocent beauty of a new series of dolphins
overtaking the craze of g-strings.

We are…
MOTION.
With ease we…
rock the boat into sending waves over seas.
Now the ocean is screwed over by rivers
damned into accepting knocked-kneed surfer bunnies
who use the waves to recite their kinda motions and poetries.
We change seasons by moving ocean tides and hiding the
moon under our glistening armpits 'til all you can do is find
your mind stained by our rolling droplets of salty knowledge.

Powered by the rise of the sun...our rays never go astray.

We keep moving even when 340ml of tardy apologies flow down your throat threatening to acidify your money-penny dreams from your insides out

and just when you thought it was your time to die or at least stop moving,

we mould swift wind out of your still, stale air,

have you soaring orange skies with mouthfuls of cloud trapped between your teeth as you inhale our scenery.

I AM...
just as fly as
YOU ARE
and since we can't stop mid-air
Motion forever
WE ARE...

[I am, you are, we are...Poetry delight]

# Fabulous!

I'm fabulous.
Forget my stunning curved legs
and inwardly turned waist,
it's just me –
I'm fabulous.

I'm no blue-eyed, blonde-haired, bamboozled barbie doll.
But I am that sun-kissed, mistake-missed, perfection-hissed,
little Miss.
Before I'm chocolate-dipped,
I am that soft, succulent, perfectly-positioned peach plotting
its fall right before luring its prey-
"Natural" some may say but I'll settle for FABULOUS any
day.

These breastisists
and sophisticated fingertips
ain't got nothing to do with it.
This It, this fabulous It,
this It that cannot be justified by being called an It.

I am as rich as the soil I tread on.
Give me just half the chance and I can turn any honest man
into a con -
artistically tryna fraud my heart away,
not knowing that line of work is clichéd; its already been
played
plus it's my game so I win anyway.

Understand that I'm way too fabulous to even tilt an afro-strand
when u holler at me from ur street corner
'coz only where there's kutlwisiso for my kinda status,
at that spot,
uzong'thola khona.

Yes!
Ghetto fabulous
with a twist of suburban scandalous.
U could come duze, baby
but I don't think u could handle it.

I hope when I smile u look into my eyes and perfection you see,
'coz if not u just missed out on an opportunity.
Opportunity of sight-seeing into my soul
and realising that maybe someday this kinda fabulousness u might know.

Before my first breath could chill my spine,
allowing me to cry for the forth-coming minute miseries of my life...
I was fabulous.
Before the act of my conception could be conceptualised...
I was fabulous.
I am fabulous before u can even fathom my fabulousness.

Before –
winds have breeze,
waves are acquainted with the seas,
or war is the opposite of peace..

Fabulousness is me.

Even before –
babies knew how to hunger;
g-strings were inspired by tangas;
or Africanism needed inyanga.
My Fabulousness, kudala ikhona!

I will remain fabulous even when my lungs fail to expand
with my soul's inhale
or the politically incorrect await aloneness for their
incorrectness to be exhaled
This fabulousness cannot be traded-in
or be given up for sale
Let me just give you an idea of what it entails-
W.O.M.A.N

Yes, Fabulous is my name,
but u can call me Woman
'coz it's one in the same.
Now with this kind of title that rocks the concept of fame to
shame,
how can I not be Oh-so-Fabuloso over and over and over
again?

[Dedicated to Mr Welsh, 2006]

# The Poet and her Habit

The poet took her overdose-
Swallowed words until she spat out verbs
and gagged on adjectives that stopped just on the tip of her
tongue
(because even the description of saliva never needs to be dry).
The poet drank a box of local intelligence;
the kind that came in 6packs and crates and altogether
amounted to 99% of intoxicating phrases
(the other 1% was the recycled clichés that came with living
on "the stuff").
Drunk, she urinated formal synonyms that smelt of colloquial
diction.
The poet inhaled idioms
and smoking metaphors filled the air.
She stuck sharp sarcasm into her arm;
She was high...
The night before,
she'd been snorting on distorted syntax
through a rolled-up note of grammar
that had chipped punctuation around its edges.
Apparently this morning she woke up hung-over
from creating antonyms out of euphemisms.
Now look at her,
trying to concoct colours by mixing tautology with similes.
The Poet –
the word junkie.
(Shame on her for expanding the boundaries of apostrophes
'cos after taking shots of verses with her,
now everyone thinks they own creativity.)

# Beads of Sweat...it's Summertime

Beads of sweat deliberated all winter long
about how they were going to construct multiple waterfalls
all over her body...
in due time.

May was their first official meeting.
May was the first time she'd wrapped a scarf around her neck
-
that's when they decided that it was time to plan.
The king of all beads of sweat shouted for a meeting from the
top of her forehead,
in a few days all of them had gathered under the scarf around
her neck -
the one she'd unleashed in May to fight off the soldiers of
chill
that surfed the winds and caused commotion from her ears to
her frozen toes.

All the beads of sweat agreed to a simple policy.
It stipulated: "In the next meeting, they would recruit -
pores ready to constrict and defend them by raising hair,
nipples willing to display harder attitudes,
blood ready to flow so far from the surface that it risked
missing out on rare suicidal and blood donation invitations."

They knew her neck was a safe place.
Their studies of her conscious showed that she could never
wrap her scarf hard enough to pressure them into pore-lands
of separate beads of sweat ethnicities and so she would never
be reason for them to fall without their consent.

So these beads of sweat planned, spoke,
had a few laughs about the pseudo-sunshine that almost
made her smile in winter-time.
They rolled in their pores in absolute stitches; swelling up
with bellies full from laughter.
This continued until the alarm went off in October.
The beads of sweat gathered in their respective places,
composed and ready to start a revolution of waterfalls
throughout that body of hers for the first time in summer-
time.

One day, just before Eos the goddess of dawn opened up the
skies for Helios to shine,
every bead of sweat took a deep breath and the moment after
they dived.

The first waterfall of sweat came from the extravagant jump
taken from the temple by the king who led by example:
He and his team streamed down her cheeks and joined her
armpit beads who were only too ready to reach the bottom of
her breast to join the others.
In just a few seconds her half-dressed body was covered in
glorious waterfalls of sweat
and she was happy to know that once again it was summer.
She listened as the screams of their joy invited blood to flow
faster,
her heart to beat healthier
and her pores to lick the salt off of their freedom.
She giggled as the last waterfall tickled the back of her knee as
it glided down her smooth shaven calf.

She was conquered by waterfalls of sweat and all she muttered as a sunray collided into her temple in an angle that started the revolution again...

all she muttered was:

Thank God it's Summer!

# Wind and her Knickers

I've decided. Sometimes I'm just going to tell my words to shut up when they don't know any better. Sometimes I'm going to let my eyes describe the image of the wind blowing the flimsy materials of her summer dress to those heights that I think make boys and me smile in hope of seeing the full-floral knickers underneath. I need to be absolutely silent to decipher why she smiles from embarrassment and would deny us the opportunity to see her full-floral knickers when she didn't dictate to the winds to blow. All we want to do is see what her morals deny us. Then, after watching how - without grace, but much attempt - she walks towards the wind, pleading with it not to whisper anything else in public, her smile fades to **insec**ure straightness. She secretly asks the wind not to blow past her again; exposing everything she was taught to hide from strangers. She strikes bargains with it. Promising to wear matching ones next time or at least ones pretty enough to be exposed by accident but **only** in case of accidents. "Next time", she prays. "Next time, I will do it right. Wear **the best set of** knickers and comply with any wind regulations you may have for me, then. **But right now,** please, leave me be. Let everyone around me forget who I am from my **knickers down.** Please stop telling them secrets about my thighs and knees and the **colours on my** panties. Please have enough mercy on me to let me be invisi**ble until I decide** to speak." But see, I can only really hear that speech **if I tell my wo**rds to shut up long enough to listen to the **images -**

83

especially those on her face and between her **curved,**
**embarra**ssed smile and its insecure **straight-**
**ness. S**o…I'm letting my words **rest so**
**that I** can see her fight to **hide her**
**knicker**s from me. I **need to**
**compre**hend the **scene**
**properly so**
**Shhhhh.**

# Baby, I Cheated

Baby I cheated.
Let me explain: You see, my love, when you weren't looking
I looked away too and I spotted him in a crowd.
I promise the crowd was big, huge, gigantic even
and seriously I wasn't searching but his gaze found mine and
suddenly…

my rose petals whiffed of a touch of pink,
my relish tasted better than the sight of the sea making love
to the sky on a summer afternoon and creating different
shades of light blue.
He lay there like he was designed for me
Can you believe his audacity?

My sweetness, I swear!
His type caught me off guard and took advantage of me.
I, who was vulnerable to his big….and tasty….
it was shaped like the kind of flavour wrapped around the
most beautiful day
and sprinkled across my bed before my body you'd lay…I
mean he'd lay.
I was confused so he figured he'd drive me insane.
Truth is, Baby, if the taste of his sugar were a bit more
delayed
I would have found my sanity and not stayed in his presence
for days.

Baby I promise I didn't mean to look anyway.
In fact, as soon as you started turning your eyes towards me,
again,

I tried to convince myself that my mother had taught me better than to stare
and that G.O.D was about to send a bolt of lightning to distract me.
But he didn't. So I carried on.
And on and on and on and…
You see, he turned me into his pebble and I cycled in his cyclone
he twirled me in his beauty and I tried to leave
but he had me stuck in his sea of…
Delectable: a not so salty sea that paralysed me into not knowing how to swim
because I got used to him making me float.

My Honey-tea, darling, I love you
but truth is if it were possible I think I'd wanna dip him in my every morning coffee
making sure he becomes putty for me before I devour him.
Sweetie, I adore you
but you know I have a fetish for dark chocolate and once I look, I have to touch
and I'm the greedy type so it's never enough.

All I'm saying is that:
Roses aren't always red
And violets don't sound like they should be blue
Tonight when you finally decide to look you probably won't find me next to you.
I'll be out cheating with big Mr. Tub of Ice-cream, chocolate-flavoured with bits in the middle…I know I said we were doing this diet together but ho e kutswa just feels too good!

# Round. Pronounced. VoLuPTuOus.

I used to define my curves by the way he squeezed my waist
or indulged in the turning of my round, PRONOUNCED
VoLuPTuOuS.
I used to see myself through his eyes -
momentarily beautiful –
dressed in a sexy that would later be conveniently undressed
for his pleasure
and then some satisfaction of my own
[So I thought]

I only knew how I smiled like that when he held my hand.
I only knew it was real when he'd understand.
I saw myself…
I saw myself as a reflection in his eyes
and refracting in his eyes was only an image that he'd defined
in me.
I saw myself as a reflection, reflecting the image *of my* window
*to my* soul
Through *his* eyes.

With every him came an every me
When he was happy, I existed contently
Until-
One day the boy caught amnesia,
Forgot who I was so I lost ME.
Through him, I lost ME.

So I set out-
Prepared a mental feast for my distorted image
told my spiritual feet that they would get weary along the way

but this was a journey I had to take.
I deliberated on whose cultural route I could follow
to discover the soil within this weary,
waiting,
wanting-to-be-a-woman
woman whom I WAS
but never knew how to Be.


I told dear heart that it was time for…ME.
I unwrapped the hands that were cupping the nipples of my soul
and breast-fed my mind with the kind of colostrum produced to make me grow
even if I wasn't bearing his offspring.
I became mother of my inner child and I taught her that-
These breasts were made to pass on wisdom to offspring
but she should not be afraid to touch them.
I told that child:
Those humps and bumps that adorn your thighs and behind
do not deserve to hide from the rays of the sun,
Love those curves and turn your mind to the splendid grooves that echo experience
and life
and YOU within them.
And when you feel that they have rightfully named your delightful turnings "cellulite"
turn to Table Mountain who takes pride
in the uneven rays of sun that try to caress her rocks and stones and patches of delightful imperfectly perfect contours,
Even she exists as more than just a pretty sight to be climbed and named and admired.

Dear Miss Mountain exists as a symbol of living from the future back to your unrecognised past.

The beautifully round, pronounced, voluptuous child smiled at the reflection she saw in a rain drop,
I looked at her happy and I recognised all that resides in me and this body.
So... I adore you dear little Miss Round. Pronounced. VoLuPTuOuS.
I do.

# Spit Fire!

Spit fire!
and breathe out smoke.
Your brain is going up in flames as you skate through new ideas
leaving the old ones covered in coal.

Spit Fire!
then inhale more oxygen.
Hold your breath and let those thoughts grow bigger
fume better.
Let your lungs and blood get used to this firey side of you.
Let the fresh oxygen find every hidden fuse
before you exhale again and...
Spit Fire!

Spit Fire!
And breathe out smoke.
Be the nasty dragon your thoughts are pushing you to be.
"Kick", "Push" and find a place where you "coast" through the new easily.
You're on stage, the dry winter grass is staring you right in the face
So…
Spit Fire!
And watch the world around you ignite in your flame.

# My Appeal

Only in my arms can my baby be rocked to sleep
even in that kind of solitude I reckon he is deep
I stare into eyes and the sparkle he tries to disguise just
magnifies
but truth he knows that I is us and he is we
can't give me a better reason to believe than this
loneliness he relieves
this shiver I receive
oh yes he is... in deed

Please don't try to convince me,
I know he does
it's me he loves
as pure as doves
and as cleansing as a disinfected all-white tub
He is my grub;
my mexican hot sub
Debonairs move over 'cos I've found my love.

"I know that he loves me cos he told me so"?
Oh hell no, I can feel that he loves me 'cos he showed me so.
But unlike most niggas that I find whack, who be tryna mack
telling me that they be feeling me like that
my baby be different because he be digging me in vernac
He tells me hore wanrata
just before antswara
and rocks lefatse laka.

Don't know if kea sicka
but ke tlo qala ho leaka if I don't catch a breather

91

He is my breath taker-awayer
buffy my loneliness slayer
*My* all-round player
and always a part of my night-time prayers.

He is my baby, my boo,
a part of my left brain too.
He collaborates with my thoughts
creating my desires.
He choirs my acquired desires
and my thoughts he inspires.
My late night fire...
my brand new tiger-wheel tyre.
Baby come over here and let us conspire!

I would call you my perfect brotha
but our actions would be condemned by our motha
With your touch that's unlike any other
Be my all-time lover?!

Come on...
you know we're more than a conspiracy
I'd be your Queen if you'd let me
come sail these seas with me
'cos in us I see more than my fantasy

Sheba.
If wa tshaba
then tshwara letheka laka
Together retla tswaka
together we'll be love-warriors and conquer the likes of bo-
Shaka.

Nkgopole like a night cap just before you go to sleep.
Just like ke ho hopola before I invite you into my dreams.

I'm in love with the infatuation your scent has caused my senses to feel.
I love missing you 'cos my attention your absence is able to steal
You see...
we are real
this thing we can't conceal
if you just constantly tell me how you feel
I'll consider this a sealed deal.
Cos see baby...
You are My Appeal

# The Story of Women's Day

A band with over 20 000 members played outside the Union Buildings.
This was the biggest protest concert our streets had ever seen,
The greatest band ever established because it featured women only
And their album title was *liberty*.

Meneer J.G might have missed the performance and forgot to personally collect his complimentary tickets signed with their autographs and messages of freedom.
But ask the little ones strapped onto their backs
they had front-row seats to the making of this history.
There were four main conductors involved in the composing of this memory;
Mme Helen, Rahima, Lillian and Sophie.

In the far left corner, Rahima Moosa led the union of women who were dressed in hope and harmonised dreams.
They had strings of all colours of the rainbow wrapped around their thoughts,
Mosadi e mong le e mong ea neng a eme moo, one a ithatetse ka letlalo la tshepo.
A hope that each one had gained after slaughtering their fears and leaving seshebo sa teng for future females who would be forced to dream
in times when papa ea bona ea tsebo would not be enough to sustain them spiritually.

A band with over 20000 members played outside the Union Buildings…

In the close right corner,
Mme Lillian Ngoyi sat recording the backing instruments to
freedom songs.
She recorded jazzy sounds of:
mother's intuitions,
Sisters' soft smiles
Grandmothers' wisdoms
As well as recipes of love as ululated by voluptuous aunties.
Mafumahadi who sat here ane ale ditswibila tsa modidietsane
ba tsanyaola in pitches that told various stories about women
who played the role of ditshiya to their people.
Empa mona they sat harmonising,
their throats vibrating at the same pace to lyrics of freedom
in the same way.


A band with over 20000 members played outside the Union
Buildings…


Mrs. Sophie Williams' place was to help choreograph the
steps
taken by those women who stood restlessly in the near left
corner.
All she had to do was witness these women with different
skin tones
hold hands and dance circles around anyone who had ideas of
undermining them.
Their steps were courageous!
Ha! The way they flung their fists in the air
made the wind shy to blow between the gaps in their fingers.
Every position taken by their arms was gracious
and complemented the strength their flexible thighs had to
endure

whenever their male counterparts needed the strength of their homes.
With every move their backs were upright, secure.
These backs were used ho pepa mathata a lefatse
and protect vulnerable hands from losing their grip on life.

A band with over 20000 members played outside the Union Buildings…

In the last corner stood the women who created lyrics
joined by and Mrs. Helen Joseph.
These women possessed voices that inspired God to build the world in 6 days
because on the seventh he just wanted to rest and listen.
Their words were made from rebellious stones
and sounded bold enough to compete with mountains.
These women's words named every mother different colours of the African sunset
and raised daughters who had Modimo as the detail of their dimples.
The lyrics sung needed nothing except a world that understands that women are rocks
no matter how chipped,
they cannot be extinct.

All four corners collaborated to the perfect song
and as they turned their backs to leave in victory,
one anonymous woman took centre stage
and looking up at every white cloud
that had ever threatened to block her sunshine
and told it who she was softly:

'Ke se tswantso sa bo ra ditebele ba tswaraneng ka matsoho a
kganathetseng bofubedu,
dipelo tsa bona tse tsweu
ba bososela dipososelo tse bonwang ditafoleng mo hodutsing
bana bareketsweng  Seanamarena ke bo ntata bona.
Ke pepa seriti sa ka fatuku emongojwana,
Fella hase hoba ke tella
Empa ke qhobeliwa ke nyenyefatso ya molao ho nwa,
Mosadi!
Ho thwe, Mosadi ha o cha o cheche.
Empa ke a latola, le kgale!
Nke ke ka  chechele morao ha lefatshe le ya pele.
Ke tla ema ka di tshetshekwane,
ke fine dibaki,
ke itahlele ka setotswana.
Mosebetse ha o fele.
Waka mosebetse ha se hodula setulong,
empa ho tswara tau ka ditlena
ke nke diqeto …

Jwale he, ke nkile qeto hore  seriti saka ke tla se phahamisa
ke se thethetse hara mpa mathata
se bonwe ke dichaba
ebe kgau ho basadi le makgabunyane a tlang ka mora rona
Ke tla se hodisa ntate,
Ke sebaballe
ho fihlella basadi bohle ba ikemela
ba ikgantsha ka bosadi ba bona
Hona he, etla ba setswantso sa di kano le dikatleho
tsa boMme bohle ba ileng ba e lwana matsoho a bona
ka kganathela bofubedu ntweng ya bokamoso ba rona.
Letsatsi le tla fihla…

empa ka leo re tla theolela re tlotle
Dikgabane tsena."

She turn to join the rest of the band of 20000 women who
played outside the Union Buildings...

(09 August 2009)

# (Lesbian) Right (in) to (Love) Freedom

Sprinkles of rain caressing my skin
(all because I refuse to take shelter under her umbrella).
Fingers intertwined under the lens of daylight
(even if she too is a woman).
Picketing outside your window last night
(but only because I exercised my right to be wrong).
Chained to nothing but her love
(so I never feel isolated for long).
Running my lips against her bare back
(because I like how my dark sits on her light).
Smiling
(because it's not a curfew keeping me locked-in at night).
Lesbian and in love... I call it my freedom, you just call it my
right.

# The Heavens are pouring and staining

It seems it's pourin' with heaven today.
Yesterday it started off as a drizzle...
the one cape town used to specialise in;
where you'd be spat on, constantly and precisely
yet just only.
Just enough for you to squint but hate the labour of carrying
an umbrella -
and when you didn't,
as you were in the middle of raising your finger to halt the
taxi,
your afro started letting you know how much it'd actually
soaked up
and it laughed close to your scalp in uneven pitches.
Still, yesterday the heavens were only leakin' -
people would shout out "amen" here and there,
some would quietly proclaim that a miracle droplet had
landed on them
while others managed to wipe the sparse blessings off their
compact foreheads.

But today...
Heaven's contents are full-on pourin'
on uneven afros, complaints, and parching fates.
The heavens are even diluting buckets of carefully-brewed
hater-aid.
It's about to be a crisis for those whose professions ask them
to bitch and moan
and punctuate sighs with never-satisfied groans.
The heavens are pourin' and stainin'
and even making those house calls to Tyrones.

From the corner of your eye
you can spot joy stains on boys who tie their sneakers with
laces of dull depression.
Everyone of 'em grumpy niggahs have these unmissable
bright stains of joy just splattered on their tugged cardigan
sleeves
and spoiled frowns that now look as happy as the colours on
autumn leaves.

And there,
straight ahead,
your faded dreams are given the kind of stains that have made
them reappear.
Now ousted even in the dark
(where you thought you'd tucked them into the corners of
your fitted sheets)
the stains just make them dreams so damn real.
It's like now they're yours again...
you thought you'd given them away
or added enough vanish
but now every time you open your eyes you see them hanging
from your eyelashes.
And every time you sleep you make more dreams
and the heavens just continue to pour.
Pourin' them thick-ass stains that taint all things that dent
your heart and tire your soul.
Stainin' all things that burden your hands
and even the teeth that take chunks out of your whole.

The heavens ain't playing today...
They're pourin' and stainin'

and soon your whole will be covered in thick-ass stains of all
things
shweet and soft and solid
and dope and light -
all things that make you high on your own life.

The heavens have leaked
and now they're pourin' and stainin'.
Leave your umbrella indoors,
with this batch of droplets
even your afro will remain happily on duty and bound to
grow.

Let the heavens pour...

# SUCKLED FROM BETWEEN FLOWER PETALS

*The flutter rests…secrets are uttered and landscapes of realities perceived*

# Peach Pit

My incisors began the ceremony.
But first my eyes preyed.
They looked at this sweet-in-summer-not-too-taut-but-not-too-lose yellow beauty.
Peach they call it
but it was about to be my meal.
My eyes had eyed it in the fridge for a span
but it's when I put it down on the kitchen table:
its hair standing on end
and the coldness of its skin flirting with the heat...
that's when my eyes knew it was time.

My incisors began the ceremony
While the wrinkles between my thumb curved around Miss Peach
as if they chanted sweaty bewitchings that would make her feel lekker gesuip,
Miss Peach approached my mouth in graceful silence.
She was
 firm yet soft
enticing yet daunting.
She was everything a married man asked his mistress to be
except she also made the perfect wife.

My incisors began the ceremony.
But it was my canines
that ripped her yellow skin from her orangeness.
Purpose
Juice
Bite

Dripped
Skin torn
Down the right side of my mouth
onto the right side of my chin
to be fetched by the wrinkles between my other hand.

My incisors began the ceremony
that only extravagant
indulgent
greedy
hungry
Greek god-prayers understand as they feast on abundance.
Even their dogs know not of left-overs.
And their poor get full off the smell alone.

My incisors began the ceremony
that parted yellow from orange
skin from flesh
piece from wholeness
yet we can never speak in lines of death or lack or injury.
Miss Peach was a pure offering
to palet
to throat
to thirst
and to the wrinkles that wiped the juice that dripped.
Again
skin was parted from flesh
and glorious flows landed between the cleavage of my thighs
this time.
Still I chewed
and closed my eyes
and thanked all Gods for abundance

and fruit
and juices
that keep my parched summer mouth moistened with...
Peach

Just when I had no more words to use to thank
I cussed;
Interrupted the trancing ceremony because my incisors met
her Pit.
hard-headed
arrogant
bitter Pit who lay in the middle of her.
Everything she was, she'd known through him
Everything I loved encompassed everything he was:
Brown
Bitter
Wrinkled
Hard
Unmoving
Unchanging

I love Peach
but Pit?
(eish)

# She's coming back

She's coming back.
And I welcome her.
She's coming back with her dreams, ambition to test their reality and experience them at the expense of rest, boredom, nervousness and self-doubt.

She's coming back.
And I welcome her.
I welcome her dreams and her sense of self that has fattened with experience of others and herself.
I welcome her learnt insecurities too because they no longer hinder her from motioning towards me.

She's coming back to me.
Coming back after years of feeling lost, of drowning in fear, of swimming in tears, and of rocking to her silence.
She's on her way back because she has found ways to believe in spite of all these things forming part of her.

She's coming back.
Coming back with her poetry, her ear for the lyrics and her sureness about the beauty of dirurubele.
She's coming back and I know because I'm with her...walking with her towards our home, our heart, dreams, and the love that taught her love.

She's coming back.
And I welcome her.

# You're cordially invited to sit next to me

For a little while…please just sit here next to me
Please sit quietly but intentionally
Just so that I can feel you near but not have to speak
I think I want to just listen to the way you breathe
And maybe even see if it's in sync with me

Maybe put your hand over mine
That would also work out just fine
But don't caress or squeeze
Just place it there (but not lifelessly)
I don't want to be distracted from feeling your warmth
Or hearing you breathe next to me

I'm not sure if I want us to be sitting in the sun or sitting on
the couch or on the bed
I'm trying to find the perfect setting that would have you
sitting next to me
But not have the environment influence what goes on in my
body, heart and head

Actually, I don't want to think about it
Just come and sit next to me when you have a moment free
All I want to do is hear you breathe
And feel your warmth next to me

I think this moment would be lovely
And it would soothe me
I think if someone took a picture of this moment
They'd see the relief in my face from you being seated next to
me.

I think you and this moment would suit me
Not just in the photograph but also in contrast to this unquiet
reality.

Just come over and sit next to me

## Pink

Nothing unnatural about pink;
The sky uses it to cry about the day leaving before it rejoices
the visit from night.

# Little Miss Valentine

Allow me to introduce you to Lady-Love, little Miss Valentine
You see, Lady-Love is not like me and you
She hates your light green and despises my bright blues
Hers is a crisp white always accompanied with a pure red
Even the 6 walls in her room are plastered with a coat of unmistakeable white
white floors and even white blinds - kept as white as the knob on her door -
Enclose the spot of pure red stained on her white floor.

## Spinach Weed

I like her burnt spinach drowned in too much delicious
cheese sauce
It smells like weed
It's not quite healthy
yet never quite enough
especially when I find my tongue courting the last bit of off-
white-leaning-on-yellow
that my fork has managed to hold onto despite its saucy
proclamations.

I like the smell of *her* weed.
It reminds me of days I will miss
and pre-empts nights around which I'm still to reminisce
I can just imagine how there'll be a day when I cry while
sitting on my bachelor bed
and there'll be no need to hide the tears from
because she won't be there to spot 'em
and ask me if I'm okay
That's going to be a sad day
A day when it doesn't smell like her kind of spinach weed
A day when I'm solely in charge of burning my own spinach
and lacing it with my own cheese sauce
I'm scared it's not going to be saucy enough
or that my spinach won't resemble the smell of her weed.

I like her weed...
And to make sure she never leaves me
I'm going to buy one pot that specifically burns
and whenever I miss her, in my spinach will go.

I know the smell of her spinach weed may not stay with me
forever
so the pot, the burn, the poem and the cheese sauce are
measures...
just in case.
I really do like the fact that she believes her spinach smells
like weed.

# Vintage

Ancient thoughts about salty residue having run down her skin as liquid,
once or maybe just twice before, she'd reminisced about Happy and felt...
But right now that's vintage.
Pencil scribbling that used to sit on the now cream-coloured paper
as symbols of life and living and concepts of being alive no longer have a seating,
They disappeared as time kept rolling its dice and left those words in a distant game of...vintage.

He catches whiffs of all the red in that single rose;
the smell of...
and...
not forgetting...
But as he unclenches his fist,
all he does is release crumbled black petals simmered in his red from their thorns.
Dead Prez professed that black roses were thornless and eternal
but he forgot to exceptionalise bleeding hands and rotten, vintage, red roses that turned black when fingers wrap too long and painfully around them.

He loses time by speaking of memories.
She... she gasps for air as her memories choke her and leave forevers in her past.

They feel them wrapped precisely around their necks with the intention of stultifying their present thus paralysing their future and leaving them to only live in...

Vintage.

# The past forever in the future

We remain woven.
Quilted into extended metaphors that forgot to seize with the ending of we.
I listen to her and I imagine the words to come from him.
I talk to him and I remember memories that never leave.

We remain woven.
The history of us cannot be destroyed because it lives in language
and I cannot abandon language so I fail to escape the quilted, interwoven histories
Our stories.

# Passed Presently

My past grabbed the bone on my ankle and spun me
'til I was too dizzy to run or think or be in my present.
My past dug its decalcified bones through my flesh and
forced me to scream
somehow, looking right into its empty rib-cage,
disappearing soul…
Its bones kept gnawing…

My past pulled the track from under me,
scrapping the bottom of my feet that couldn't bleed
'cos even when I had had the chance to learn how to  feel
genuinely
I had missed that teaching
now I didn't deserve such imagery.
I fell, but couldn't bruise my knees because I was unworthy.
Still my past grabbed me
and shook me from my sole then leaned over as if to kiss my
temple.

Just when I felt my past's decomposing breath sweep past my
temple
my present thoughts of power bled out in greedy clots
and all ambition about the future was squeezed of its oxygen.
My brain shut down as secrets from my past switched it off
from its main source:
Its [subjected] Truth.
I cried unanimatedly because I stood knowing nothing.
I had nothing for coming generations,
I had nothing for my babies,
I had nothing for me.

No knowledge,
no knowing
because I'd chosen to look within myself for all the fabricated answers
but hadn't quite completed the quest of understanding my composition.

I let the decomposing breath in…

All my solid perspectives were blown up into nothingness.
As I paid attention to the life in the decomposing breath
my past began breathing into my ears.
When I stopped fighting and thinking and pretending to know:
I watched omniscient men turn illogical because they just didn't listen.
I witnessed witchdoctors being cursed by newborns who knew better than to know it all.
I saw presidents being ruled by air
and empty, damp books stunk up libraries because there was nothing there
…Nothing presently there.

I had to let my past breathe its last breath into me.
Without it, my future present would be empty.
My past passed knowledge presently.

# RevolUtion

This revolUtion will not be televised, will not be televised, will not be televised.[1]

To you, it will be advised -
pull a Houdini right in front of your eyes,
as you walk down the street
it will imprint itself on the hands of the people you greet,
you'll find it lurking, hiding underneath your sheets.
This revolUtion accepts no defeat:
it puts itself on repeat
until you can see past your own deceit.

This revolUtion will not be televised.

It will not be televised in fear of being moulded into a Hollywood feature.
No-one can show it to you;
not your grandmother
nor your high school teacher,
go ask your preacher,
chances are, a bag of ambiguity he'll spoon out and feed ya.
The paparazzi couldn't get snaps even if they tried,
'cos not even in the tabloided truth of lies
does this revolUtion want to lie.

This revolUtion will not be televised.

But, to you, it will be publicised -

___

[1] Homage to Gil Scott-Heron's *The Revolution will not be televised* and Sarah Jones' *Your Revolution*.

pull a Houdini right in front of your eyes
shock you like an expected surprise
satisfy your cravings and add an extra side of fries.
Your curiosity will be thoroughly enticed.
But no special billboard stunts -
This revolUtion is not looking for a marketing front:
No lumo colours, photoshopped pictures
nor fading images can capture this.

This revolUtion is waiting for you to realise:
YoU will not be televised!
YoU will not be televised!
YoU will not be televised!

# A Prayer

Dear Creator

We may have different perceptions about who exactly we think you are but the wiser of us know you exist, for no human mind could conjure up even the mere concepts of what and all you have created.

You have created... us. Humans who exist as pots of your perfection: spiced with faults yet scented with possibility. Help us brew ambition, simmer hope, taste like love and look like the-best-we-can-be.

The younger of us may not know enough. The elder might have forgotten most. But even in our naiveties, arrogance and forgetfulness, let us not be absent-minded or ignorant to love. Help us love all who are to grace our souls, every family member who is to make an impact, good or bad, and let us love ourselves.
And, in so doing, let us love you.

# You are not forsaken

You are not forsaken.
Not when the sky has wept blood-stenched rains to make
sure you never have to bleed again from your eyes or your
heart
or your smile covering your drowning soul.

You look to the sky and forget to see hope lightning through
thick grey clouds of darkness.
You've let salty water blind your sight for so long that your
eardrums no longer catch the rhythm of thunder,
you just hear bolts of beats making friction with specks of
sadness that tend to land in your eyes, fractioning your sight.
It's all in your mind.

You are not forsaken.
That drop of drizzle is just the beginning of life fertilizing
your mind
with promise of rainbows wrapping around your lips
and blowing kisses to mountain tops.

# baby Silence

Shh…
Silence sleeps inside the belly of Death making her bloat,
She's about to explode.
Heard the other day that her water broke
So she's about to flood the world, give birth and make us choke on
Silence.

Mama Death is about to expose her insides
That are to be feared more than the wrinkles under her wicked smile.
After she goes into labour,
The sound of the world's breathing will subside and make way for life to die.
If you have tears,
Now is the time to cry
'Cos after Baby Silence is born your vocal cords will be torn,
The sound of rolling tears will be born into nothing but
Silence.

The only way to keep Baby Silence at bay is to keep silent,
So shh…
Let Death and her baby sleep a little while longer before it's time for the essence of their lives to suffocate our lives.
Shall we have a moment of silence to celebrate our lives?
Shh…
Silence.

# Dressed as Death

And warts came splashing out of my skin until I drowned in
puss and blisters shied away from the scabbing of my palms.
My soft hands had turned into cardboard boxes housing the
ticks from a stray-dog who had forgotten its home.
I am the blood-stained streets that drive cars to inject
themselves with more fuel of death.
I am the essence of an aroma sponsored by gasoline.
If dark came in a form,
it would come dressed like the image you see
and the empty resting in my eyes.

# another Life gone.

We scientists speculate that energy really does transfer and that her flesh will feed the soil as it decomposes.

We ethnics hope that an ancestral world parallel yet connected to ours is where her spirit will find itself so that she can be one of the spiritual beings looking down on us and completing the traditional trinity.

We christians pray that god has opened up the gates for her and won't tease her closer only to redirect her to the kingdom operated by Satan. We pray that she repented and was forgiven.

We alternatives feel that she will come back to life in another form that reflects the worth she built in this lifetime.

We skeptics believe that we know not what happens and if nothing else, we hope that she knew this enough to actually live her life.

Either way, another life is gone.
Lost to those who live in her life time, lost to those who felt her alive.

Another life is substituted for an ellipsis…

[RIP Mama Lulama Walaza, 2010]

# Undoing MY Threads…MUST Be Crazy!

The loose thread of my factory-quality heart was spotted.
The little kid bastard innocently pulled on the thread and I'm becoming undone…
knit by industrial-machine knitted knit.
I'm fucking coming undone, so fragilely undone that the wind is blowing me from myself.
My thread is being carried by wind that I cannot even see but I feel it,
as I come undone, as I unthread,
as my sanity plays hide and seek with the rest of me that seeks to find so much.
What am I without my substance
without my thick woollen threads that are supposed to be tightly and intentionally crotched through each other so that I exist as more than thread on floor underneath dirt?

I've worked too hard to keep the buttons intact,
to have the embroidery - untainted by time- stay timeless.
I have worked too damn hard to be more than thread on thread, knit on knit, stitch on stitch…
that's why the thread can't be pulled any further.

I'm intact.
In fact that little piece of thread that threatened my sanity by following the wind's blow
makes me look a bit boutiquish
Like I'm perfectly imperfect and perfectly inclined to be of worth and compete with raw silks that slide off shaven legs.
Blow thread!

Play around in the wind's whispers and entice the little kids who spot and pull you.
Just know you belong to me.
Even when you playfully threaten to leave
you're a part of me...completely.

# Unpunctuated ending

He turned
full stops into flowers
so how was I to punctuate
our ending?
We went on…

# It's not over 'til the Fat Lady Sings

It's not over 'til the fat lady sings.

So the day our hearts stopped holding hands
I was on the lookout for mountains of hips and
marshmallows of cheeks
that were bound to vibrate with the moving of her Vienna
lips.
Through my wells of tears
I made sure my sight had enough leverage to scout out the
cookie monster
who was about to confirm that I'd lost my chocolate chip
that day our hearts' hands broke it off
I thought our heart-shaped rusk was about to be beaten into
crumbs or a death even worse
[like being dipped in her sweet tea or waiting to be eaten later
from the bottom of her purse].

They said it's not over 'til the fat lady sings…

So with every step that my jelly-knees knocked away from
you
I kept guessing her
tune.
I imagined her to sing something high-pitched;
the kind of note that would dig a ditch into a keyboard
and instruct the deaf conductor
to ask her voice to soar even higher
until even heaven's skies cried
(higher) until the glory of sunshine became crucified

and the black pitch from the grey clouds could only be
broken by lightning in the sky.
But that was in my mind.
So I carried on with my carrot-fed eyes
in the dark of my night because...

It's not over 'til the fat lady sings.

And there…
my pumpkin fears reappeared
as I saw this mother of obesity struggling to walk
but her vocal cords trembling directly at me.
I stood still as if ice had frozen my body into a coma
but allowed my mind to brew in a ginger of paranoia
only later to get drunk on thoughts of being alone.

Dear Miss Cholesterol came closer.
Her voice was as beautiful as I hadn't imagined it to be.
It was the spreading of margarine on a hot toasted piece;
It was the smell of coffee roasted to a kind of blend that was
sure to awaken me.
Fat Lady's throat vibrated even in the dark of my night
And I hated it.
But damn that tune sounded like peaches dipped in heaven-
flavoured cream.

Then suddenly
As I was about to gracefully accept that dear Fat Lady had
sung
So our end had just begun-
She stood still-
Only touching my left baby finger,

And it was there that I figured…

Fat Lady wasn't singing!

Her place was just to hum to the songs of that skinny man
who had disappeared into the shades of her mountainous
hips

as they walked the streets.

So question is:

Is it not over because Fat Lady didn't sing

Or is it over because she's been married to this skinny man
for so long;

maybe in their union they became ONE

so just as he sings, she hums

and it's been over all along?

Or am I still to wait for Fat Lady to break out into her solo
song?

I can't be sure because you know what they say…

It's not over 'til the fat lady sings.

Printed in the United States
By Bookmasters